To Parents and Teachers:

We hope you and the children will enjoy reading this story in English and Spanish. It is simply told, but not *simplified,* so that both versions are quite natural. However, there is a lot of repetition for practicing pronunciation, for helping develop memory skills, and for reinforcing comprehension.

At the back of the book, there is a simple picture dictionary with key words as well as a basic pronunciation guide to the whole story.

Here are a few suggestions for using the book:

• First, read the story aloud in English to become familiar with it. Treat it like any other picture book. Look at the drawings, talk about the story, the characters, and so on.

• Then look at the picture dictionary and repeat the key words in Spanish. Make this an active exercise. Ask the children to say the words out loud instead of reading them.

• Go back and read the story again, this time in English and Spanish. Don't worry if your pronunciation isn't quite correct. Just have fun trying it out. If necessary, check the guide at the back of the book, but you'll soon pick up how to say the Spanish words.

• When you think you and the children are ready, try reading the story in Spanish. Ask the children to say it with you. Only ask them to read it if they seem eager to try. The spelling could be confusing and discourage them.

• Above all, encourage the children and give them lots of praise. They are usually quite unselfconscious, so let them be children and playact, try out different voices, and have fun. This is an excellent way to build confidence for acquiring foreign language skills.

First paperback edition for the United States, its Dependencies, Canada, and the Philippines published 1998 by Barron's Educational Series, Inc.
Text © Copyright 1998 by b small publishing, Surrey, England.

International Standard Book Number 0-7641-5127-4   Library of Congress Catalog Card Number 98-72553
Printed in Hong Kong   9 8 7 6 5 4 3 2 1

What's for supper?

¿Qué hay para cenar?

Mary Risk
Pictures by Carol Thompson
Spanish by Rosa Martín

BARRON'S

We're making supper tonight, Mom.

Esta noche vamos a preparar la cena *nosotros*, mamá.

It's going to be a surprise.

Va a ser una sorpresa.

Do we need cheese?

¿Necesitamos queso?

Yes, we need cheese, and ham too.

Sí, necesitamos queso y también jamón.

Do we need flour?

¿Necesitamos harina?

Yes.

Sí.

What about potatoes?
Do we need them?

¿Y patatas?
¿Necesitamos patatas?

No, we don't need potatoes.

No, no necesitamos patatas.

But we need tomatoes
and mushrooms.

Pero necesitamos tomates y
champiñones.

Let's put some olives in it!

¡Vamos a ponerle unas aceitunas también

Oh no! I don't like olives.

¡Oh no! No me gustan las aceitunas.

How much is all that?

¿Cuánto es todo?

What are you going to make?
Please tell me. Please!

No! It's a surprise!

¿Qué van a hacer?
¡Vamos, díganmelo! ¡Por favor!

¡No! ¡Es una sorpresa!

Here we are home again.

Ya estamos de vuelta en casa.

Don't come into the kitchen, Mom.

No entres en la cocina, mamá.

Supper's ready. It's…

La cena está lista. Es…

a pizza!

¡una pizza!

Pronouncing Spanish

Don't worry if your pronunciation isn't quite correct. The important thing is to be willing to try. The pronunciation guide here is based on the Spanish accent used in Latin America. Althought it cannot be completely accurate, it certainly will be a great help.

• Read the guide as naturally as possible, as if it were English.

• Put stress on the letters in *italics,* e.g., ko*see*na.

If you can, ask a Spanish-speaking person to help and move on as soon as possible to speaking the words without the guide.

Note: Spanish adjectives usually have two forms, one for masculine and one for feminine nouns. They often look very similar but are pronounced slightly differently, e.g., **listo** and **lista** (see next page).

Words Las palabras
lass pal-*abrass*

to cook supper
preparar la cena
praypah-*rahr* lah *say*na

onight

sta noche

a nocheh

urprise

a sorpresa

sorpraysa

heese

l queso

keh-so

am

l jamón

hamon

lour

a harina

areena

omato

l tomate

tomah-teh

potato

la patata

lah pa*tah*-ta

olive

la aceituna

lah asay-*too*nah

mushroom

el champiñón

el champeen-*yon*

pizza

la pizza

lah *peet*-sah

ready

listo/lista

leesto/leesta

home/house
la casa
lah *kah-sa*

Mom
mamá
mam*ma*

Dad
papá
pa*pah*

kitchen
la cocina
lah ko*seena*

yes
sí
see

no
no
noh

please
por favor
poor fa*vor*

A simple guide to pronouncing this Spanish story

¿Qué hay para cenar?
keh ay *par*-ah say-*nar*

Esta noche vamos a preparar
*ess*ta *noch*eh *v*amoss ah praypah-*rahr*

la cena *nosotros*, mamá.
lah *sayn*a nos*s*otross, mam*m*a

Va a ser una sorpresa.
vah ah sair oona sor*pray*sa

¿Necesitamos queso?
nessessee-*t*amoss *keh*-so

Sí, necesitamos queso y también jamón.
see, nessessee-*t*amoss *keh*-so, ee tamb-*yen* ham*on*

¿Necesitamos harina?
nessessee-*t*amoss a*ree*na

Sí.
see

¿Y patatas?
ee p*at*ah-tass

¿Necesitamos patatas?
nessessee-*t*amoss p*at*ah-tass

No, no necesitamos patatas.
noh, noh nessessee-*t*amoss p*at*ah-tass

Pero necesitamos tomates
pair-ro nessessee-*t*amoss tom*ah*-tess

y champiñones.
ee champeen-*yon*ess

¡Vamos a ponerle unas aceitunas también!
*v*amoss ah pon-*air*leh *oon*ass asay-*toon*ahs tamb-*yen*

¡Oh no! No me gustan las aceitunas.
oh noh, noh meh *goos*tan lass asay-*toon*ahs

¿Cuánto es todo?
*kw*an*to ess *to*do

¿Qué van a hacer?
keh van ah as*sair*

¡Vamos, díganmelo! ¡Por favor!
*v*amoss, *dee*-ganmehlo, poor favor

¡No! ¡Es una sorpresa!
noh, ess *oon*a sor*pray*sa

Ya estamos de vuelta en casa.
ya est*am*oss deh *voo-el*ta en *kah*-sa

No entres en la cocina, mamá.
noh *ent*ress en lah kos*een*a, mam*m*a

La cena está lista. Es...
lah *sayn*a ess-*tah lees*ta, ess

¡una pizza!
*oon*a *peet*-sah

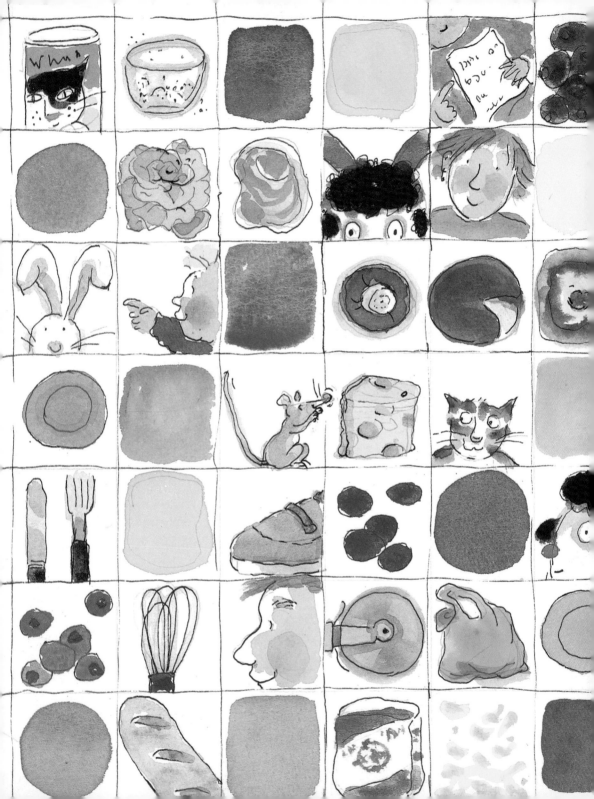